APPALACHIAN TRAIL

Fog shrouds this section of the Appalachian Trail near Sunup
Knob in Great Smoky Mountains National Park.

APPALACHIAN TRAIL

Photographs by Michael Warren

Text by Sandra Kocher

GRAPHIC ARTS CENTER PUBLISHING COMPANY

Portland, Oregon

For all those who made the
Appalachian Trail possible.

ISBN, Regular Edition 0-912856-45-9
ISBN, Deluxe Edition 0-912856-46-7
Library of Congress Catalog Number 78-75107
Copyright © 1979 by Graphic Arts Center Publishing Co.
2000 N.W. Wilson • Portland, Oregon 97209 • 503/224-7777
Editor • Douglas A. Pfeiffer
Designer • Robert Reynolds
Printer • Graphic Arts Center
Binding • Lincoln & Allen
Printed in the United States of America

The Trail passes a forsaken house standing in dormant, winter woods near Groseclose, Virginia.

Clouds surround 5,500 foot Big Bald (1,676 meters). The Trail winds down from Big Bald and passes through this upland field situated above Street Gap.

WILDERNESS IS TWO THINGS

Wilderness is two things—fact and feeling. It is a fund of knowledge and a spring of influence. It is the ultimate source of health — terrestrial and human.

—*Benton MacKaye*

"Enchanted forest" was the recurring phrase that we found scrawled in hiker's hand on the finger-worn sheets of the register at Chairback Gap Shelter along an especially wild section of the Appalachian Trail in northern Maine. It was late August, and the backpacking hikers who had left their handwritten comments in the lean-to register were, for the most part, headed north to Mount Katahdin, northernmost peak of the 2000-mile Appalachian Trail.

Some hikers who'd signed the register had walked all the way from the southern beginning of the Trail in Georgia, others were hiking in Maine for a week or more, and still others had started from various points along the Trail to the south. Almost all had stopped at Cloud Pond, where the next shelter to the south is located, and it was that stretch of trail between the two shelters that many declared enchanted. Pure romanticism perhaps, or simply cheerful observations born of good weather. Nonetheless, my interest aroused, I persuaded my hiking companion, Mike, whose photographs appear in this book, that a visit to Cloud Pond was in order.

And so the following morning, again unbelievably sunny and clear, found the two of us on our way up a seldom used trail which began about a mile and a half from the east end of Long Pond, where we'd spent the night at Chairback Mountain Camps. We expected this trail, marked by sparsely placed blue blazes, to intersect with the Appalachian Trail on the mountain ridge above us. For the Appalachian Trail is more than a single continuous trailway stretching from Maine to Georgia; it is a whole system of trails, including an elaborate network of side trails.

These side trails provide access to the Appalachian Trail at hundreds of points along its extended route. They are particu-larly useful for day hikers. Side trails climb to summits the main trail may bypass; they lead to circuits around waterfalls and to outstanding viewpoints well-worth the extra steps off the A.T. proper. (The Appalachian Trail is affectionately known as the "A.T." by those who tread its footway.) Still other side trails guide one to shelters and much sought-after springs. One could spend a lifetime exploring the blue-blazed side trails of the Appalachian Trail system.

Our trail leading up from Long Pond was atypical in that it was so little used its maintenance had lapsed. We had to push our way through surprisingly rough undergrowth, often head high. For awhile it was a game of seek-and-find as we tried to locate each blue blaze, casting our eyes from one tree with its pale blue marker through the thick stand of hardwoods to the next tree with a welcome patch of blue. It reminded me of being bow lookout on a sailing boat, navigating cautiously through the fog, searching for one guiding buoy, then another. But as we climbed higher, the underbrush thinned out and in the more open woods the trail became much easier to follow. Before long we happily stepped out upon the Appalachian Trail.

It was like meeting an old friend again, reaching this familiar footpath with its identifying white blazes. If we turned left and followed the Trail north, we'd be headed in the direction of Monument Cliff, where the first blaze for the A.T. in Maine was made in 1931, then on over Columbus and Chairback Mountains, site of our previous day's hike with its many eye-stretching views. And should we continue on toward White Cap Mountain and beyond, we would find ourselves in a moist, moss and spruce-covered wilderness, the Trail skirting shores of ponds and lakes with names like Jo-Mary, Pemadumcook, Nahmakanta and Rainbow. Ultimately we would reach Mount Katahdin. It is a wild stretch with only an occasional logging road intersecting the Trail.

Instead, we set our hiking boots to the south, choosing to cover the short distance to the junction with the side trail to Cloud Pond. Evidently no one had been over the Trail here in the last day or so, for several times we encountered displays of deep yellow and orange mushrooms crossing our footway. We knelt down to examine and photograph the umbrella-shaped forms amid the soft, spongy green moss. No doubt this was part of the enchanted forest. Soon we turned toward Cloud Pond — two-tenths of a mile to its shelter there. Balsam firs crowded close together, their lower limbs dark and needleless where little sunlight penetrated. It was a perfect setting for a gnome's dwelling or a place for keeping secrets.

It was Labor Day weekend, and at the lean-to overlooking Cloud Pond we found three boys in their early teens enjoying a last fling of summer freedom before school began for a new year. Having said hello, we left them to their whittling and meal preparation, and headed down to the shore of the pond. The sky was still clear; not a cloud punctured the blue, much less obscured the pond. We were fortunate. We'd known friends who had hiked into Cloud Pond through pouring rain, when the narrow trail edging the small oval-shaped pond was a treacherous footway over slippery rocks.

Refreshed by a quick swim in the pond's clear, cool water, we climbed out on a large rock not far from shore to dry in the sun and eagerly consume the lunches we took from our packs. A few dragonflies danced over the water's surface. It was truly a place and a moment to savor. We would be as reluctant to leave this wild mountain setting as the schoolboys, who knew Labor Day marked the termination of their own hiking and camping on the Appalachian Trail.

If we had chosen to continue hiking south on the Trail that day, rather than indulging in our sojourn into Cloud Pond, we would have been well on our way over Barren Mountain with its long ridge and ruggedly steep descent. Continuing south, the A.T. leads over the Bigelow Range, Saddleback Mountain, up over Old Speck and through awesome Mahoosuc Notch to the cloud-piercing White Mountains of New Hampshire.

Traveling southward over the Appalachians, the Trail passes through twelve more states before it finally reaches its southern terminus: the summit of Springer Mountain in Georgia. In its 2000 miles (plus 30 to 50 miles depending on yearly relocations of short stretches) the Appalachian Trail goes through two National Parks (Shenandoah and Great Smoky Mountain), eight National Forests, two National Recreation Areas, and two National Historic Parks (Harpers Ferry, and the C&O Canal). In addition, it crosses considerable state, local, corporate and private lands where its route has been established through various kinds of agreements.

As originally intended, the Appalachain Trail is essentially a mountain peak and ridge trail. It ranges in elevation from near sea level, where the Trail crosses the Hudson River, to its highest point atop Clingmans Dome in the Smokies—6,642 feet (2,024.5 meters). Where the Trail must descend into gaps and valleys, it may cross farmers' fields, follow dirt roads and at times paved ones — from country black-top to speedy superhighways. Occasionally the A.T. passes right down the main street of a small town.

But the aim is to keep the Trail a wilderness footpath and to minimize paved trailway. With the passage of the Appalachian Trail Bill in March 1978, the federal government has authorized funds to obtain land through which the Trail passes, now in private hands, and to restrain development bordering the Trail. The goal is to create a protective corridor of at least 125 acres per mile of trail and to reroute the Trail away from roads wherever possible.

Bolstered by this federal assistance and the heightened environmental sensitivity of the thousands of hikers who tread its way, that long thin strip of wilderness we call the Appalachian Trail may survive well into the 21st century. Such are the facts. The feeling is: long may its forests continue to enchant!

BENTON MACKAYE'S LINEAR PLANNING TRIUMPH

The Appalachian Trail is conceived as the backbone of a super reservation and primeval recreation ground covering the length (and width) of the Appalachian Range itself, its ultimate purpose being to extend acquaintance with the scenery and serve as a guide to the understanding of nature.

— *Benton MacKaye*

The Appalachain Trail is a great linear park, a serpentine footway over some of the oldest mountains on earth, and through some of the richest vegetation of hardwoods, conifers and flowering plants to be found in a temperate climate. Hidden within its green and rocky recesses is a wealth of wildlife too. Hikers may see deer and on occasion bear, fox, beaver, moose in the north, and perhaps wild boar in the Smokies. Smaller creatures abound, especially squirrels and chipmunks. And birds, for which the Trail is a haven, reward those who walk slowly and listen.

The man, in whose mind and imagination the Appalachian Trail was born, was a Harvard-educated forester, philosopher and regional planner named Benton MacKaye. MacKaye was a tall lanky New Englander who was born in Stamford, Connecticut in 1879 and died in 1975. He made Shirley Center, Massachusetts his home for much of his long life. As a boy he enjoyed taking "expeditions," as he called them, through the town's surrounding woodland, carefully observing the local topography and wildlife.

After receiving both the B.A. and M.A. degrees from Harvard, MacKaye joined the U.S. Forest Service in 1905 when it was first being organized under the remarkable Chief Forester Gifford Pinchot. In his studies for the Forest Service and in a plan prepared for the Department of Labor in 1918-19, MacKaye concerned himself not only with the sound conservation of natural resources but also the wise use of human resources. The working and living conditions of American workers, particularly those in outdoor occupations—loggers, miners and farmers—as well as soldiers returning from World War I, received MacKaye's special attention. He was developing a keen social-minded approach to forestry and planning.

MacKaye knew the White Mountains of New Hampshire and other mountains in the Appalachian chain. He was well versed in matters of forest growth and the flow pattern of rivers. Yet he spoke just as easily of the flow patterns of people; how, for instance, people flowed from an urban nexus such as Times Square in New York City. His language was very visual, very graphic. "The regional planner, like the architect and the engineer," MacKaye wrote, "is a visualizer. His plan is a picture, a picture of possibilities."

Thus it is not surprising that there came to Benton MacKaye the image of a trail extending the length of the "Appalachian Domain" as he called it. (On occasion it became "Appalachian Empire.") It would be the backbone of a great linear reservation, a trail within reach of the majority of people residing in the urban centers of the eastern United States.

The year was 1921 and the time was ripe for the idea of an Appalachian Trail. The setting for a meeting of receptive minds was Hudson Guild Farm in Netcong, New Jersey. It was there, in July of 1921, that Benton MacKaye joined his friend Charles Harris Whitaker, editor of the *Journal of the American Institute of Architects*. Whitaker introduced him to an architect named Clarence S. Stein, who chaired the Institute's Committee on Community Planning.

MacKaye's thoughts on a trail which would follow a wilderness belt of the Appalachians, from a prominent peak in the north to the highest peak in the south, caught Clarence Stein's imagination. Stein urged MacKaye to write up his proposal, which he did, and the now historic document "An Appalachian Trail — A Project in Regional Planning" was published in the *Journal of the American Institute of Architects* in October 1921.

Two years later, again at the Hudson Guild Farm, MacKaye, Whitaker and Stein joined social critic Lewis Mumford, planner Henry Wright and others in founding the Regional Planning

Association of America. They were idealistic men who were familiar with British garden cities. Their planning thought incorporated a sensitivity to human scale, community values and the importance of green open space. MacKaye added his special dimension of a strong geographic sense.

The Trail itself was, of course, the paramount feature: the heart of MacKaye's 1921 proposal for "an Appalachian Trail." On a map accompanying his original article, the projected trail was shown extending from Mount Washington (in New Hampshire) to Mount Mitchell (in North Carolina) with several branch trails feeding into this main trail. The trail would incorporate already existing trails wherever possible, including those in the White Mountains of New Hampshire and part of the Long Trail in Vermont's Green Mountains, begun back in 1910. Elsewhere the trail would be laid out and constructed in sections by local groups.

MacKaye envisoned the trail as a place where people laboring away in cities could retreat for a true uplift in body and spirit. Dividing landscape into three complementary parts: primeval, rural, and urban, he felt strongly that people needed to experience the primeval. To facilitate summer living on and near the primeval environment of the trail, MacKaye proposed a series of shelter camps—enclosed huts offering meals and sleeping space along the trail—similar to the popular system of huts which the Appalachian Mountain Club continues to provide today.

Besides the shelter camps, MacKaye pictured a series of community camps near the trail. These would be recreational communities for summer living with land held in common. And with the further thought of providing food for the shelter and community camps, MacKaye went on to recommend the establishment of cooperative food and farm camps located in adjoining valleys or on farmland near the community camps. We must remember that he proposed these various camps and the trail itself at a time when much of the terrain over which the trail might be laid was truly wild and undeveloped.

Trail shelters, some enclosed but most of a three-sided lean-to

design, were constructed as an integral part of the Appalachian Trail—and they remain so today. Unfortunately, many suffer the problems of overcrowding and misuse, especially where they lie near the reach of roads. Neither the community camps nor the food and farm camps were implemented. Perhaps it was just as well, as MacKaye himself later realized, for in time they too would have threatened the wilderness integrity of the Trail.

Nonetheless, these proposed community-oriented camps reflected MacKaye's social philosophy: 1) that the Trail be accessible to people, 2) that non-speculative land use undergird the various communal camps (and the Trail itself, he later emphasized), and 3) that there are positive values inherent in close community exchange. Looking back on MacKaye's contributions, following his death at the age of 96, Lewis Mumford perceptively observed, "The Appalachian Trail was indeed a dramatic social idea."

The Knife Edge, Mt. Katahdin.

CONSTRUCTING A TRAIL THROUGH THE APPALACHIAN EMPIRE

By dramatizing the long trail as the key to the Appalachian Empire, as he loved to call it, MacKaye incited hundreds of others to participate in the laying out of the route, achieving by purely voluntary cooperation and love what the empire of the Incas had done in the Andes by compulsory organization.

—*Lewis Mumford*

Certainly there were other trails before the Appalachian Trail — informal foot-trails, Indian trails, trails of the westward pioneer migrations. The trail is part of American history. And in the East there were other hiking trails before the one MacKaye proposed. The Crawford Path up Mount Washington, which dated from 1819, initiated a series of trails in the White Mountains. The Long Trail through the Green Mountains of Vermont originated in 1910. By the early 1920s, a large portion of this 266-mile Long Trail — from the Massachusetts line to the Canadian border — was well underway.

From time to time, avid hikers and knowledgeable men of the mountains had proposed extended trails. But no one before MacKaye had conceived of a major continuous trail spanning the entire north-south route of the Appalachians, tying together existing trails and creating hundreds of miles of new trail. It was a fresh, farsighted and exciting idea.

The lure of the Appalachians themselves should not be discounted. They are mountains rich in natural beauty, in the fascination their geology and biology holds, and in their associated human history. All conspired to make the very name "Appalachian Trail" an electric force. A force that galvanized a remarkable host of people — largely volunteers, but also employees of the U.S. Forest Service and National Park Service. Together they contributed their knowledge, time and physical energies to the construction of the longest marked footpath in the world.

The Appalachian Trail came into being within just a little over a decade — from 1922, when the first stretch of new trail was built in New York State, to the Trail's initial completion in 1937. The feat is all the more amazing when one considers that many sections of the Trail had to pass through what was then largely unexplored wilderness. Certainly the Trail's early heroes were those men who undertook the scouting and routing of the Trail. Their familiarity with specific mountain areas contributed immeasurably to the piecing together of a viable route over the ranges and peaks of MacKaye's "Appalachian Empire."

In 1922-23 the first newly constructed portion of the Appalachian Trail — from Bear Mountain Bridge south to the Ramapo River below Arden, New York — became reality. It was followed the next year by completion of the section from Arden to Greenwood Lake. Meanwhile, in the southern reaches of the Appalachians, exploration went on to determine a fitting southern terminus for the Trail. For it had been decided to carry the Trail farther south than Mount Mitchell, just as in the north, the projected trail was extended to Mount Katahdin.

After considering several peaks in Tennessee and Georgia, Mount Oglethorpe in the Amicalola Range was selected. Its summit, crowned with a marble shaft commemorating the founder of the Georgia colony, remained the southern terminus of the A.T. until 1958, when commercial developments forced a relocation to Springer Mountain, about 23 trail miles to the northeast. And so Springer now stands as the southernmost peak of both the Blue Ridge and the Appalachian Trail.

Inevitably there came into being an organization to coordinate the work of the numerous Trail planning and building groups springing up the length of the Appalachians. In 1925, at a meeting in Washington, D.C., the Appalachian Trail Conference was founded. The Conference still serves, in greatly expanded fashion, as the coordinating body for the A.T.

Despite the initial creation of this Conference in 1925, little action followed in the ensuing months. It was still up to a small group of highly motivated individuals — those early Trail heroes

—to step forward and push the Appalachian Trail into existence. One of those men was Arthur Perkins, a retired lawyer from Hartford, Connecticut, who in 1926 resuscitated the languishing Trail project and gave it the impetus needed to move forward.

Perkins in turn drew into the Trail's planning and construction orbit a man named Myron H. Avery, then living in Hartford. In so doing, Perkins brought to the physical creation of the Appalachian Trail probably the single most dynamic individual to be associated with the Trail's realization. Originally from Maine, Avery soon moved from Hartford to Washington, D.C., where he helped to establish the very active Potomac Appalachian Trail Club. In the routing and construction of many sections along the length of the Trail, Avery proved to be a man of strong personality. He was the sort who managed to overcome seemingly insuperable obstacles, often inspiring others to do likewise.

With the various initial routes for the Trail established by the early "Trail heroes," the trail crews then set to work. Strong men with limited equipment (saws, bush clippers, crowbars and such as could be packed in), they cut through overgrown vegetation, cleared away fallen trees, moved rocks to improve the footway and built primitive bridges over streams and swampy areas. They also constructed shelters for overnight use, measured distances and made signs to mark intersections.

Perhaps most importantly, the Trail builders gave the A.T. its visual identity: the blaze of white paint brushed on trees and rocks to guide the seeking hiker. (Today a uniform 2 by 6-inch vertical white rectangle prevails.) Arthur Perkins designed a 4-inch diamond-shaped metal marker as well, emblazoned with the **A** logo of the Trail. Above treeline, stone cairns serve as talismans of the hiker's way, symbols of true alpine climbing.

In perusing the written progress reports of those early years of the Trail's routing and construction, many of which appeared in *Appalachia,* bulletin of the Appalachian Mountain Club, one catches beyond the matter-of-fact reportage, some of the force and flavor of the A.T.'s construction scenario. For example, Arthur Perkins wrote in 1928:

In Maine about twenty-five miles of trail from the Great Basin of Katahdin to Ripogenus Dam, were scouted and marked by members of the Appalachian Mountain Club's August Camp on the west side of Katahdin.

In Vermont the Dartmouth Outing Club and the Green Mountain Club undertook the construction of a connecting trail from Hanover, N.H., to Deer Leap, near Rutland, Vt. This was completed with the exception of about six miles, work being interrupted in the fall by the floods. When it is finished the Appalachian Trail will be complete from Grafton Notch in Maine, to Blackington, Mass., just north of Mt. Greylock.

Out of the energetic trail building efforts of the 1920s and 30s, many hiking clubs evolved in different regions of the Appalachian East. Among these, there emerged the Blue Mountain Club in Pennsylvania, followed by the Potomac Appalachian Trail Club, the Georgia Appalachian Trail Club, and — in the wake of some especially difficult but ultimately successful trail routing and construction — the Maine Appalachian Trail Club founded in 1935. Also the Appalachian Mountain Club, with a history dating back to 1876, actively contributed its share of trail work. Today this Club maintains almost 200 miles of the Trail.

The Appalachian Trail is a living, ongoing entity. There are nearly fifty hiking and outdoor clubs, some of them college outing clubs, who join the National Park Service and the U.S. Forest Service in maintaining specific sections of the Trail itself. They also maintain hundreds of miles of blue-blazed side trails, the shelters and, when necessary, engineer trail relocations. It is a continuous operation, fueled largely by volunteer hands.

From its headquarters in historic Harpers Ferry, West Virginia, the Appalachian Trail Conference coordinates the work of these member Trail clubs and fosters beneficial state and federal assistance for the Trail. It acts as the clearing house for major decisions on Trail relocations and other aspects of Trail management. The Conference publishes the official Trail guidebooks with their detailed maps and the *Appalachian Trailway News.* Also, to this busy headquarters come visiting hikers and Trail enthusiasts from all over.

ON AND BEYOND THE TRAIL

To walk down the Blue Ridge: to be alone: to exert and strain up and down hills under a pack: to see the 'thin green slice' of the eastern green deciduous forests: to search for a consciousness unencumbered by front page graffiti and the daily pressure of the city. Time and space to relax and tune to the rhythm and demands of the land.

—John Seidensticker, "A Letter From the Appalachian Trail"

The Appalachian Trail attracts the hiker who is also a seeker. It offers an objective, a beginning and an end, whether it be for a day of hiking, a weekend on the Trail or several weeks of backpacking. For some it even offers its whole 2000 miles, an end-to-end challenge. Hiking is a highly kinetic experience: with your body you feel the landscape in a way no other experience can duplicate. The Trail is exacting. It can demand much of you; it can test your body's endurance, it may torment you, it may expand your soul.

The A.T. has its own geographical definitions—nature and the early Trail builders saw to that — and you must hone to them. Mountain after mountain is there to challenge your every step, streams may quench your thirst or they may lead you to a slippery fall over their mossy rocks. The Trail is a microcosm of a particular kind—a strip of Appalachian wilderness awaiting you. Within it you may increase your knowledge of rocks and minerals, of woodland wildflowers, of almost endless species of trees and plants, of birds and their calls. And as your visual and kinetic senses are expanded, so also is your sensitivity to sounds and smells. The sound of the wind, of a loon calling over a remote Maine pond, a moose crashing through the underbrush; the odor of wet leaves or balsam firs…

The Trail may test your sense of direction, map reading abilities and digestion of guidebook information. It may tell you something about your own inner need for solitude. Or, at the other end of the scale, your ability to be sociable — in a crowded lean-to or as a leader of 20 twelve-year old backpackers fresh from urban settings. In any case, the A.T. will tantalize and challenge, educate and frustrate. In the end its visual beauty may remain with you for years to come, triumphant over memories of being soaked to the skin in days of unrelenting rain or overwhelmed with swelling bites of the North's black flies of spring and early summer.

To Benton MacKaye, the great visualizer, the Appalachian Trail offered a means of studying the primeval environment firsthand. It rewarded those *with eyes to see.* The visual evidence was there, he felt, to understand the geological evolution of the mountains, the genesis of a forest. I, too, collect visual images along the Trail, much less scientifically induced than those of MacKaye, but no less valued.

On busy days far from the Trail when I want to relax, I call upon these visual images, gold nuggets as they were, collected over the years from many hikes on the Trail in different regions and seasons. Often I see myself atop a sunlit grassy bald in the southern Appalachians. It is late June, and Mike and I are enjoying a restful stop just off the Trail, lying on our backs with heads resting on our day packs as pillows.

I love these open grassy balds where, for reasons scientists are still trying to determine, a pasture-like openness prevails. If we sit up, amid the sea of grasses, we can see the flowering yellow hawkweed, buttercups, some tiny bluets and, joy of joys, wild strawberries, laden now with tiny sweet berries—soft red morsels that melt in your mouth. We hike slowly over the balds at strawberry time.

Other images of innumerable day hikes on the Appalachian Trail crowd in. I see—and feel again—a cold blustery day in early April when we climbed Blood Mountain in Georgia — up from Neels Gap. It was colder than the New England we'd left a few days ago! Even the upward climb failed to warm us, and the enclosed stone shelter on the summit offered a welcome respite from the chilling wind. We stayed inside long enough to share some hot tea with another hiker who was backpacking his way north.

I also see the broad Lehigh Valley in Pennsylvania spread out below us with its early summer patchwork of fields and farmhouses. We've just hiked in to Bake Oven Knob Overlook on a warm, rather hazy day. (Clambered in really, over a sea of rocks.) If nothing else, one learns in hiking these Appalachians that mountains are made of rock — especially from Pennsylvania northward! Sharp small rocks, slippery rocks, sliding rocks, rocks of old stream beds which now serve as trailway. Boulders that one must hoist one's self and pack over — or in-between. Rock. We somehow propel ourselves upward. The summits are waiting.

We are on top of Mount Rogers, highest peak in Virginia. Yet trees shade the summit. There is no distant view. A heavy damp mist hangs over the summit forest of red spruce, the trunks hoary with moisture and moss. I am momentarily transported north to New Hampshire and Maine, land of more spruce. There, bare summits and rock ledges open out to a vast world all around in an undulating flow of cloud-streaked peaks and ranges. It is as close as one gets to nature's heaven.

Another visual nugget. Autumn in western Connecticut. Following the Trail along the banks of the broad, flowing Housatonic River near Cornwall Bridge. Away from the river in adjacent fields, cornstalks still stand, tawny and stiff after several hard October frosts. Nearby we wander toward an old abandoned farmhouse, its former yard overgrown with dried grasses and milkweed. The pods of the milkweed, dark in the late afternoon sun, appear like long black mouths exuding cotton fluff.

The next day up on St. John's Ledges, still in Connecticut, autumn spreads before us in a quiet quilt of yellows, reds and greens in the valley below. Autumn both exhilarates and saddens. I covet its short-lived days of golden glory, even in rain — which seems to heighten the rich colors all the more. Fall blows away on a windy night and denuded trees usher in November's spare, brown cloak. But with the approach of winter, more vistas open up again along the Trail, the foliage curtain having fallen for another season.

Reeling ahead: a late winter nugget. We are hiking up on snowshoes to Little Rock Pond in Vermont. It is midday; a light snow is falling but the trees along the Trail filter the snow to a light dusting of white on our red and blue parkas. Finally the trail reaches the Pond. Why, we can walk right over the snow-covered ice to the small island in the pond! On that island there was once a lean-to with a small footbridge leading over to it. Overuse led to the removal of both lean-to and footbridge some years ago. But the island is still a delight to explore—on snowshoes, or barefoot on a hot summer's day after swimming over to it.

Winter is long in the mountains, and I greet spring all the more heartily each year. In Virginia's Shenandoah region, I love the contrast between the open winter-brown woods and the delicate colors of early spring wildflowers. White bloodroot with yellow center, the violet ranging from its namesake hue to pale yellow and white, a whole hillside of pink trillium nodding at us. Winter's seal is broken. Down in the valley, shadbush spreads its pink-tinged white blossoms amid the feathery yellow-green of neighboring trees coming into leaf.

Hiking on the Appalachian Trail's forest route is punctuated from time to time by the Trail's passing through small villages and towns — towns we might otherwise have missed — each given a special status by the presence of hikers on its streets. Hot Springs, North Carolina; Damascus, Virginia; Duncannon, Pennsylvania; Monson, Maine...

And rural America. The Trail crosses many a pasture, often leading the hiker over stiles or through gates which one must be careful to lock again, lest the cattle wander astray and the goodwill of the Appalachian Trail be lost. Once we hiked right through a farmyard as the A.T. followed a narrow road up from Eckville, Pennsylvania, toward the Pinnacle. From the barn issued a woman carrying a basket of eggs, freshly gathered from her hens. A closer view than one would see on a Sunday drive.

History. The Appalachian Trail leads you through it. Quietly and often quite unobtrusively. Around the Carry Ponds near the Kennebec River in Maine, Benedict Arnold (still loyal to the colonial cause) traveled up the river and over many a portage in

1775, intent on surprising the British at Quebec. The region is still called the Carrying Place. Today a set of sporting camps with that same name welcomes not Arnold and his men, but hungry hikers who, for a reasonable rate, may eat pancake breakfasts to their heart's content, a scant three-tenths of a mile from the Trail.

Soldiers who cross mountains are a hardy breed, and the Overmountain Men from Watauga Settlement in North Carolina (now Tennessee) were no exception. Refusing to swear loyalty to the British crown, the militia of over 1000 men followed Bright's Trace through Yellow Mountain Gap near Roan Mountain while snow was falling in September 1780. A sign posted on the Trail by the Tennessee Eastman Hiking Club commemorates the crossing through the gap by the mountain militia on their way "to victory at King's Mountain." The aim had been to forestall a British major and his men who were intending to join forces with General Cornwallis coming up from the south.

For hiking Civil War buffs there is, most dramatically, old Harpers Ferry, West Virginia, just off the Trail and now under the aegis of the National Park Service. The era of John Brown's raid and the ensuing war comes alive in the town's striking architectural and natural setting above the confluence of the Potomac and Shenandoah Rivers.

There is social history, too, to be discovered along the Appalachian Trail, again in quiet, half-hidden places. In Pennsylvania, at Rausch Gap, the Trail passes near an old cemetery. Once a whole town flourished there, complete with railroad passing through. Today only a set of gravestones languish in the forest setting, reminders of that town of the past.

And up the hollows of the southern Blue Ridge, hikers may come upon the sagging remains of log cabins. Perhaps only the chimney still stands, the log portion having long ago burned down. Lush vegetation crowds in on the evidence of human habitation. A few rangy apple trees alone may indicate the former presence of a backwoods farm.

It is well that the Appalachian Trail has been designated a National Scenic Trail by a Congressional Act, which was signed by President Lyndon B. Johnson in 1968. (In the West, the Pacific Crest Trail was also given this special status.) And, as we know, the more recent Appalachian Trail Bill of 1978, under President Jimmy Carter's signature, authorizes funds for a protective corridor bordering the Trail. It is an act of promise; the appropriations are yet to come. But the promise has been made to the American people. The long linear slice of Appalachian wilderness has great hope of continuing to serve hikers flocking to its mountain domain.

The Appalachian Trail is both reality and symbol. A rugged 2000-mile footpath with endless miles of side trails feeding into it. A place and a space to get in touch with nature and with oneself. I have heard young and old hikers on the Trail, and those who have never seen the Trail (many from the Midwest), remark, "Before I die, I want to hike the entire Appalachian Trail." For them the Trail is a symbol of fulfillment. May it continue to be so. In the hope of capturing some of the visual reality of the Appalachian Trail, as well as its symbolic spirit, this book has evolved.

Aspen leaf, Lower Jo-Mary Lake.

This sign, surrounded by a hiking party, marks the northern
terminus of the Appalachian Trail on Baxter Peak,
Mt. Katahdin, 5,267 feet (1,605 meters).

A group of hikers heads toward South Peak from Baxter Peak.
Thoreau, impressed by the lofty heights of Katahdin, called it a
"cloud factory." At the far left is the Knife Edge.

Dusk settles over Daicey Pond in Baxter State Park as the last
rays of the day bathe Mt. Katahdin. Right: The trees on Barren
Mountain display a rich tapestry of autumn colors.

Weathered trees stand guard over East Chairback Pond.
Left: Early morning mist rises above Long Pond. Hikers
may visit the pond via one of several side trails.

A bull moose feeds during the late afternoon on aquatic plants
in Pugwash Pond, near Gulf Hagas.

Leaves carpet a stretch known as the Arnold Expedition
Portage Trail. Here an army, under the command of Benedict
Arnold, passed through en route to Quebec in 1775.

Looking toward West Peak from Myron H. Avery Peak on
Bigelow Mountain. In 1931, Avery initiated a survey to develop
a route for the Trail in Maine.

Fungi, lichen and moss form an intricate pattern on a fallen log
alongside the Trail near the East Branch of Black Brook.

Tall grasses sway in the wind below C Pond Bluff. Right:
Overhanging trees drop their leaves along the bank of Frye
Brook as autumn begins to wind down.

The East Branch of Black Brook cascades over rocks and boulders; a refreshing reward after descending Elephant Mountain. Left: The impressive Bigelow Range looms above Maine's Carrabassett Valley.

Canadian dogwood in spring bloom south of Saddleback
Mountain. Also known as bunchberry, this plant displays red
berries in summer.

In the Presidential Range, known for inclement weather,
the wind, clouds and sun play tag around the peaks of
Mts. Washington, Monroe and Eisenhower. At 6,288 feet,
Mt. Washington (1,917 meters) is the highest mountain
in the northeastern United States.

A hiker trudges through the snow on Mt. Jackson in
White Mountain National Forest.

The Trail wanders up the barren ridges of Mt. Lafayette to its
5,249 foot summit (1,600 meters), the highest peak in the
Franconia Range. Mt. Lincoln is the distant peak.

Clouds momentarily part, revealing the steep cliffs of
Whitewall Mountain in Zealand Notch.

From Lonesome Lake, peaks of the Franconia Range crowd
the distant horizon.

Birch and maple line the Trail through Zealand Notch. Here,
the Trail follows an abandoned logging railroad grade.

Hikers explore open rocks on the summit of Mt. Liberty, a
short distance off the Trail.

The sun heralds the end of day as it sets over a field to the west
of Moose Mountain. Killington Range looms on the horizon.

A weathered barn, complete with a hand built rock wall, nestles
in a verdant meadow near the village of West Hartford.

Stratton Pond, a favorite destination for hikers, lies below
Stratton Mountain. Right: Random patterns of beauty abound
in Benton MacKaye's "Appalachian Empire."

Cheshire Village spreads out below the Cobbles. The white
spire of the First Baptist Church adds a dominant New
England note to the town. Left: Early morning mist rises over a
cemetery in the small, rural town of Tyringham.

After traversing the Housatonic Valley, the Trail crosses the
summit of Mt. Everett. Early settlers to the region referred to
Mt. Everett as the "Dome of the Taconics."

The bright leaves of the maple and birch proclaim the
culmination of fall on the north slope of Bear Mountain.

Dense foliage shades the banks of the Housatonic River as it
flows southward, eventually emptying into Long Island Sound.

Not far from Cornwall Hollow, spring violets add a touch of
color to the moist green woodland floor.

The Trail reaches its lowest elevation, near sea level, here
where it crosses the Hudson River on Bear Mountain Bridge.
New York City is less than 40 miles down river.

Winter's subtle colors linger into early April at a small pond
along the Trail near Dennytown.

A late afternoon sky over Island Pond in Palisades Interstate
Park (Harriman Section). It was in this region that the first
portion of the Trail was built during the early 1920s.

The stark lines of a winter forest are reflected in the waters
of Longhouse Creek near Upper Greenwood Lake.

A thousand foot descent via a side trail leads hikers to
spectacular Buttermilk Falls.

South of Sunfish Pond, the Trail crosses over Dunfield Creek,
which eventually empties into the Delaware River.

Autumn reflections shimmer in Lake Lenape, not far from the
village of Delaware Water Gap.

Sunlight sharpens the silhouette of Mt. Tammany as the Delaware flows through the Gap below. This vista is from Lookout Rock on Mt. Minsi, part of the Delaware Water Gap National Recreation Area.

Morning sunlight filters through the mist and trees near the
Schuylkill River in Port Clinton.

In winter, the George W. Outerbridge Shelter overlooking the
Lehigh Valley is a welcome sight.

The Trail winds around the Kessel, following the ridge until it
descends to Swatara Gap. The snow covered farmland below is
part of the Lebanon Valley.

The Susquehanna River and the village of Duncannon lie
below graffiti covered Hawk Rock on Cove Mountain.

The confluence of the Shenandoah and Potomac Rivers at
Harpers Ferry, as viewed from the Maryland Heights. Right:
The fertile farmland of the Cumberland Valley stretches
beneath the open ledges of High Rocks.

A typical residence in Harpers Ferry. The town is also
headquarters for the Appalachian Trail Conference.
Left: The vantage point of Jefferson Rock so impressed
Thomas Jefferson that he wrote: "The passage of the Potomac
through the Blue Ridge is perhaps one of the most stupendous
scenes in nature."

Dogwood foliage highlights a misty fall day south of Keyes Gap
near the Virginia-West Virginia border.

From Marys Rock in Shenandoah National Park, the broad
expanse of the Shenandoah Valley unfolds below. The
Massanutten Range serves as a backdrop.

The Trail winds around Blackrock in the southern section of
Shenandoah National Park.

White-tailed deer cross the Jones Run Trail near its junction
with the Appalachian Trail.

Hawthorn berries glisten on a rainy day north of Rockfish Gap.

The tiny, sweet morsels of the wild strawberry reward the
hungry hiker on Loft Mountain.

Winter blankets the Trail. Devils Knob and Humpback
Mountain are visible in the distance.

The James River winds its way through the Virginia Blue Ridge
toward the Piedmont. This vantage point is from the Trail as it
crosses Little Rocky Row.

Upper Crabtree Falls cascades past shadbush (also called
Allegheny serviceberry) in George Washington National
Forest. Right: Wild phlox bloom luxuriantly on Cole Mountain.

From this vantage point high on Big Tinker Cliffs, farms can
be seen in the Catawba Valley far below.
Left: Lichen adds a distinct texture to the Dragons Tooth, a
fascinating rock formation in Jefferson National Forest.

One of the more than 200 shelters along the Trail, Pine Swamp
Shelter is notable for its stone construction.

From an outlook on Big Walker Mountain, a patchwork of field
and woodland graces the southwestern Virginia countryside.

The many fingers of Watauga Lake, a TVA impoundment,
spread out below Iron Mountain.

Winter settles over a small farm in a hollow beneath Hump
Mountain along the Tennessee-North Carolina border.

Catawba rhododendron *(Rhododendron catawbiense)* in full
bloom amid Cloudland Gardens on the summit of Roan
Mountain, 6,285 feet (1,916 meters).

Near Big Bald, the Trail wanders through a sea of fringed
phacelia *(Phacelia fimbriata)*, a flower native to the
southern Appalachian Mountains.

The Nolichucky River, whose Indian name means rushing
water, cuts through the Pisgah and Cherokee National Forests.

Looking south from Mill Ridge, winter's quiet beauty abounds.

Ice forms a delicate pattern on a farm pond several miles from
the town of Hot Springs.

Spectacular trail construction on the south slope of Mt. Cammerer in Great Smoky Mountains National Park.

Spence Field, a few miles before the Trail turns south toward
Fontana Lake and the Little Tennessee River.

Aptly named, flame azalea *(Rhododendron calendulaceum)*
brightens the woods and balds of the southern mountains.
Here, a cluster blooms forth on Cheoah Bald.

From Wayah Bald in Nantahala National Forest, morning mist
mingles with a sea of mountains. Nantahala is Cherokee for
"Land-of-the-Noon-Day-Sun."

Winter conditions make travel on the Trail arduous, as on this
stretch along Shuckstack Mountain.

The familiar 2 by 6 inch vertical white blaze marks the Trail
through Bear Pen Gap.

The limb of an oak tree repeats the pattern of the ridges in this
view from Bly Gap on the North Carolina-Georgia border.
Georgia is the southernmost of the fourteen states through
which the Trail passes.

On Rocky Mountain in Chattahoochee National Forest, a slope
is highlighted by a bold display of autumn foliage.

On the Trail, hikers descend into Hightower Gap near Hawk Mountain. Springer Mountain is less than a dozen miles away.

Looking westward from the 3,782 foot summit of Springer
Mountain (1,153 meters). This peak is the southern terminus of
the Appalachian Trail and has a register with hikers' names and
comments, such as "All the Way!"

This bronze plaque marks the end of the Trail. It is one of
three plaques along the Georgia Section of the Appalachian
Trail and was made in the early 1930s by members of the
Georgia Appalachian Trail Club.

A trail of about nine miles leads hikers down Springer
Mountain to Amicalola Falls State Park. It passes near
the head of Amicalola Falls.

The Appalachian Trail is the longest continuously marked footpath in the world. Spanning fourteen states, this 2,000 mile trail runs down the Appalachian Mountains from Maine to Georgia.

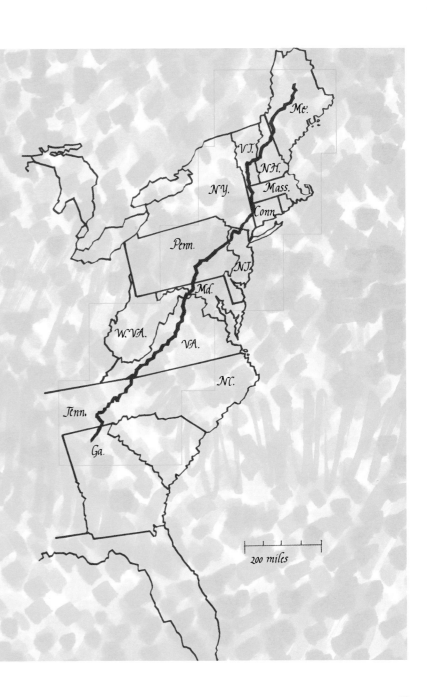

200 miles

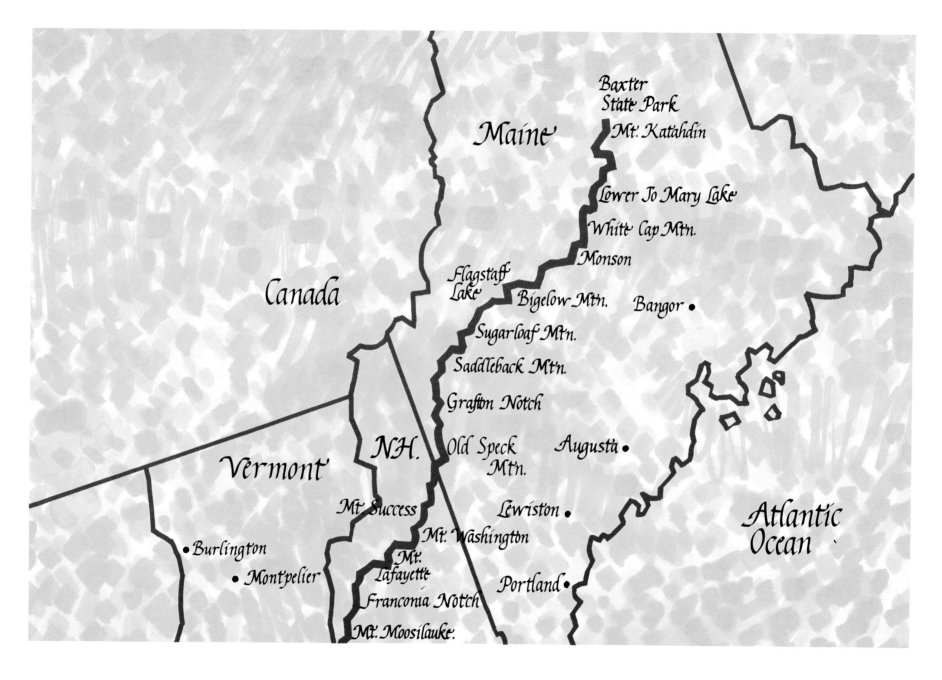

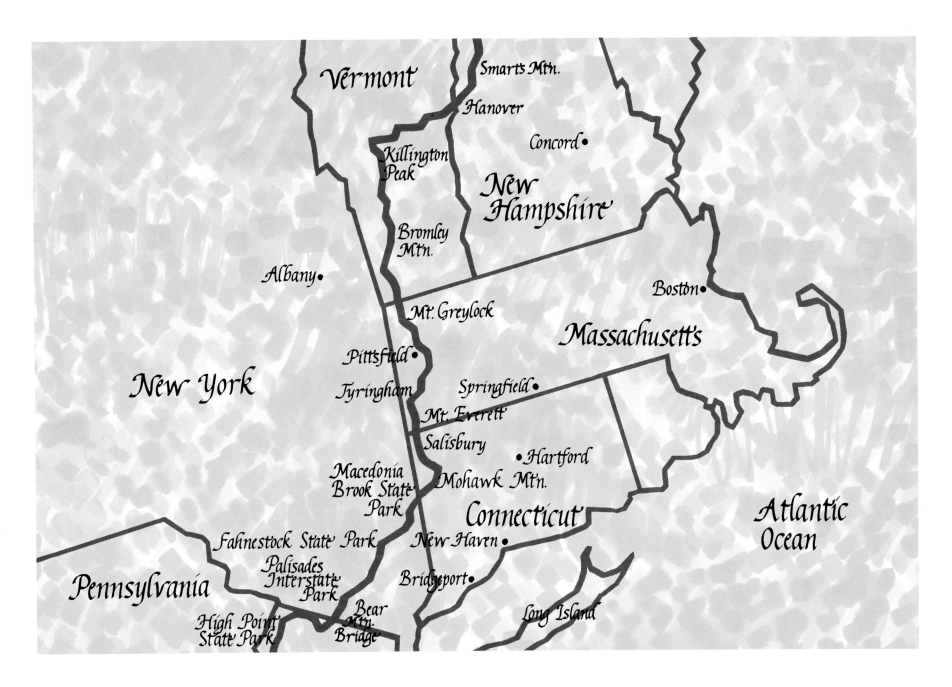

Vermont

Smarts Mtn.

Hanover

Concord

Killington
Peak

New
Hampshire

Bromley
Mtn.

Albany

Boston

Mt. Greylock

Massachusetts

New York

Pittsfield

Tyringham

Springfield

Mt. Everett

Salisbury

Hartford

Macedonia
Brook State
Park

Mohawk Mtn.

Connecticut

Atlantic
Ocean

Fahnestock State Park

New Haven

Palisades
Interstate
Park

Pennsylvania

Bridgeport

Bear
Mtn.
Bridge

Long Island

High Point
State Park

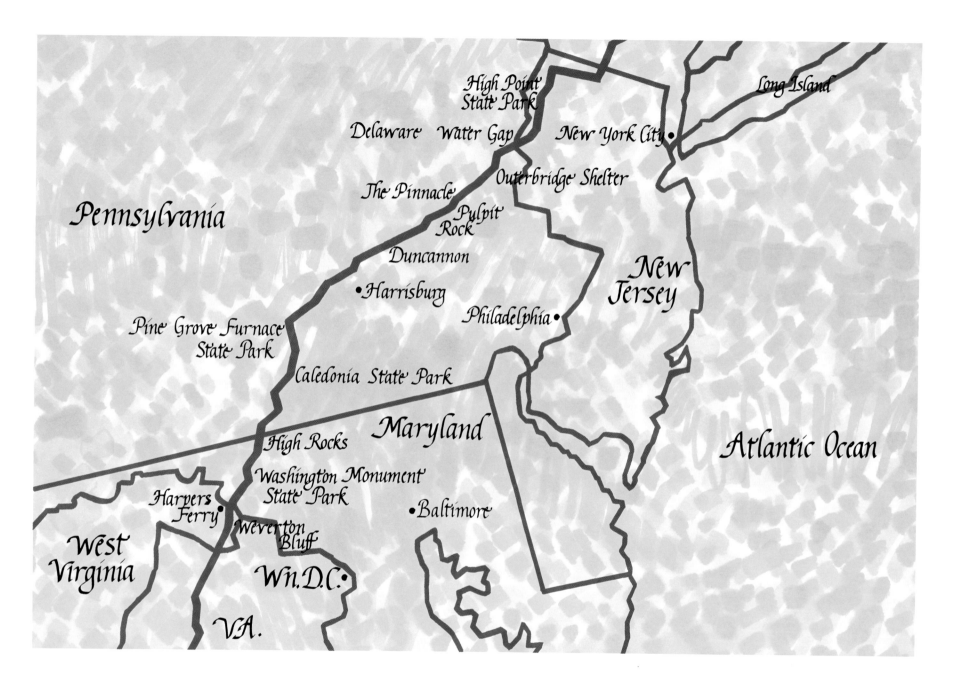

High Point
State Park

Long Island

Delaware Water Gap   New York City •

Outerbridge Shelter

The Pinnacle

Pennsylvania

Pulpit
Rock

New
Jersey

Duncannon

• Harrisburg

Philadelphia •

Pine Grove Furnace
State Park

Caledonia State Park

Maryland

Atlantic Ocean

High Rocks

Washington Monument
State Park

Harpers
Ferry •

• Baltimore

West
Virginia

Weverton
Bluff

Wn. D.C. •

VA.

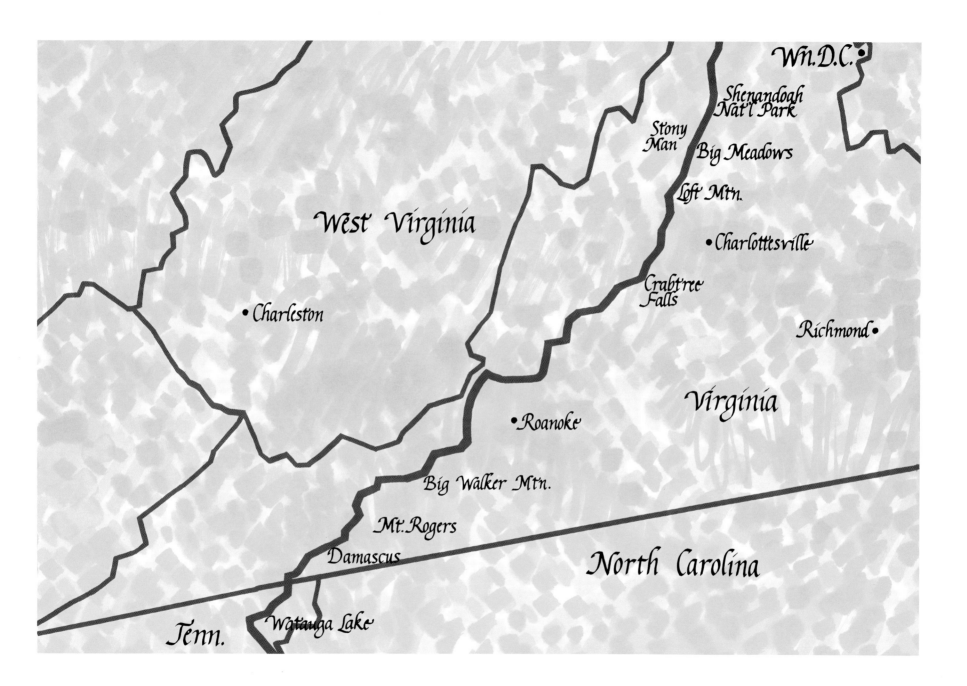

Wn. D.C.•

Shenandoah
Nat'l Park

Stony
Man   Big Meadows

Loft Mtn.

West Virginia

•Charlottesville

Crabtree
Falls

Richmond•

•Charleston

Virginia

•Roanoke

Big Walker Mtn.

Mt. Rogers

Damascus

North Carolina

Tenn.   Watauga Lake

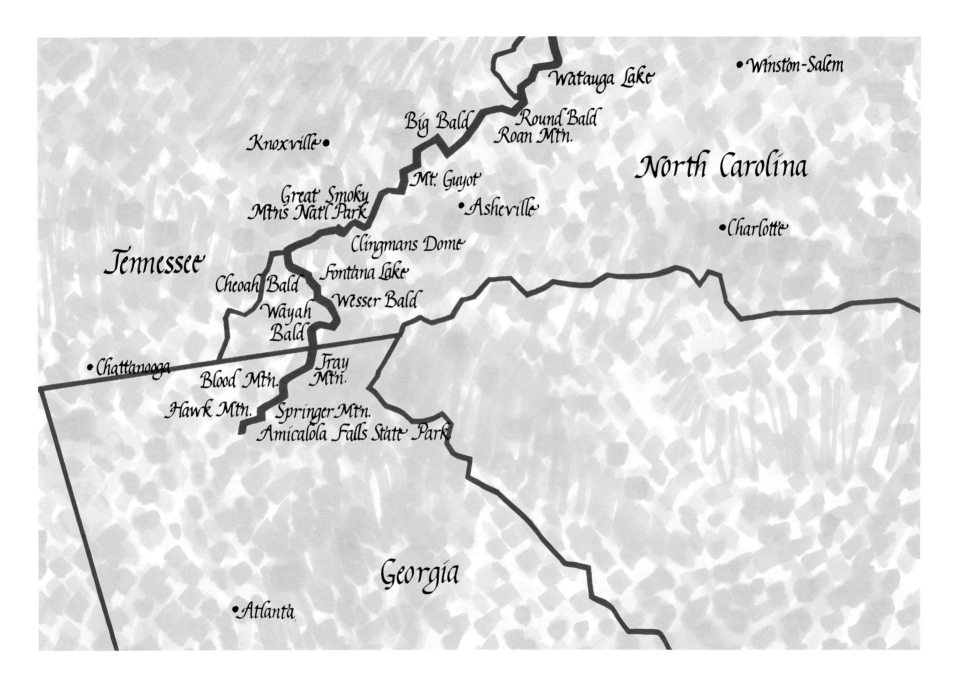

Winston-Salem

Watauga Lake

Big Bald   Round Bald
             Roan Mtn.

Knoxville

North Carolina

Mt. Guyot

Great Smoky
Mtns Nat'l Park   •Asheville

Tennessee   Clingmans Dome

                    •Charlotte

Cheoah Bald   Fontana Lake

Wayah   Wesser Bald
Bald

•Chattanooga

Blood Mtn.   Tray
              Mtn.

Hawk Mtn.   Springer Mtn.
Amicalola Falls State Park

Georgia

•Atlanta

ACKNOWLEDGEMENTS

We are grateful to the publishers of the following works for permission to reprint selections from copyrighted works:

From "The Appalachian Trail: A Guide to the Study of Nature," *Scientific Monthly* vol. XXXIV by Benton MacKaye. Copyright © April 1932 by the American Association for the Advancement of Science.

From "Dam Site vs. Norm Site," *Scientific Monthly,* vol. LXXI. Copyright © October 1950 by the American Association for the Advancement of Science.

From "Outdoor Culture: The Philosophy of Through Trails," *Landscape Architecture,* vol. XVII. Copyright © April 1927 by Landscape Architecture.

From "Benton MacKaye as Regional Planner," *The Living Wilderness,* No. 132 by Lewis Mumford. Copyright © January 1976 by the Living Wilderness.

From the introduction to *The New Exploration* by Benton MacKaye. Copyright © 1962 by the University of Illinois Press.

From "Progress of the Appalachian Trail," *Appalachia,* vol. XVII by Arthur Perkins. Copyright © June 1928 by Appalachian Mountain Club.

From "A Letter From the Appalachian Trail," *Appalachian Trailway News,* vol. 37 by John Seidensticker. Copyright © September 1976 by Appalachian Trail Conference.